Powerpoint

PDF
Audio
Video
eBook
Podcast

Scan Me

Grammar Practice Worksheets

Copyright.

This publication contains English grammar in various forms and levels. This publication is intended to be used as a supplement to other educational content. This publication is a general English resource and should not be considered as an authoritative publication. As with all educational resources, there is no guaranteed result implied from the use of this resource. The English grammar in this publication is a brief overview of certain parts of the English language.

The publishers hope this publication will assist all users in their language learning journey. Every attempt has been made to create a general knowledge resource. This publication in no way is intended as an authority on any subject including English grammar. Every effort has been made to offer English grammar as it is generally understood. We hope you are able to study and learn English from our publication.

Index

Part One

English Fundamentals Worksheet

Alphabet

There are **26 letters** in the English alphabet.

There are **5 vowels**: **A, E, I, O** and **U**. The rest of the letters are **consonants**.

Practice reading the letters out loud:

Capital letters (upper case letters):

A B C D E F G H I J K
L M N O P Q R S T U
V W X Y Z

Small letters (lower case letters):

a b c d e f g h i j k l m n
o p q r s t u v w x y z

English Fundamentals Worksheet
Writing the Alphabet 1

Copy each letter of the alphabet into the box below: Lower case (or small) letters:

a	b	c	d	f	e	g	h	i	j	k	l	m

n	o	p	q	r	s	t	u	v	w	x	y	z

Upper case (or capital) letters:

A	B	C	D	F	E	G	H	I	J	K	L	M

N	O	P	Q	R	S	T	U	V	W	X	Y	Z

English Fundamentals Worksheet
Writing the Alphabet 2

A a   B b   C c   D d   E e   F f   G g

H h   I i   J j   K k   L l   M m   N n

O o   P p   Q q   R r   S s   T t

U u   V v   W w   X x   Y y   Z z

English Fundamentals Worksheet
Personal Details

Practice writing your personal details with this form:

Please use capital letters

Mr/Mrs/Miss/Ms: _____

First Name: _____

Surname: _____

Address: _____

Post Code: _____

Telephone Number: _____

Mobile Number: _____

Email Address: _____

Age: _____

Date of Birth: _____/_____/_____

Nationality: _____

Occupation: _____

Marital Status: _____

Number of Children: _____

English Fundamentals Worksheet
Basic English Written Test

Name: _____

Date: _____

Days of the week:

_____

_____

_____

_____

_____

_____

_____

Months of the year:

_____

_____

_____

_____

_____

_____

_____

_____

_____

_____

_____

_____

Numbers 1-30:

1. _____
2. _____
3. _____
4. _____
5. _____
6. _____
7. _____
8. _____
9. _____
10. _____
11. _____
12. _____
13. _____
14. _____
15. _____
16. _____
17. _____
18. _____
19. _____
20. _____
21. _____
22. _____
23. _____
24. _____
25. _____
26. _____
27. _____
28. _____
29. _____
30. _____

English Fundamentals Worksheet
Essential Spellings

a b c d e f g h i j k l m n o p q r s t u v w x y z
A B C D E F G H I J K L M N O P Q R S T U V W X Y Z

Sunday, Monday, Tuesday, Wednesday, Thursday, Friday, Saturday
January, February, March, April, May, June, July, August, September, October, November, December

spring, summer, autumn, winter

0	zero	18	eighteen
¼	quarter	19	nineteen
½	half	20	twenty
¾	three quarters	21	twenty one
1	one	10	ten
2	two	20	twenty
3	three	30	thirty
4	four	40	forty
5	five	50	fifty
6	six	60	sixty
7	seven	70	seventy
8	eight	80	eighty
9	nine	90	ninety
10	ten	100	one hundred
11	eleven	101	one hundred and one
12	twelve	1,000	one thousand
13	thirteen	1,001	one thousand and one
14	fourteen	10,000	ten thousand
15	fifteen	100,000	one hundred thousand
16	sixteen	1,000,000	one million
17	seventeen	1,000,000,000	one billion

English Fundamentals Worksheet
Vocabulary Test

Write_____starting with each letter of the alphabet.
For example: _____.

A _____   N _____

B _____   O _____

C _____   P _____

D _____   Q _____

E _____   R _____

F _____   S _____

G _____   T _____

H _____   U _____

I _____   V _____

J _____   W _____

K _____   X _____

L _____   Y _____

M _____   Z _____

English Fundamentals Worksheet
Days, Months & Seasons 1

Fill in the gaps to spell the names of days, months and seasons:

1. _ _ i _ a _

2. O _ _ o _ e _

3. _ _ u _ _ _ a _

4. A _ _ i _

5. _ e _ _ u a _ _

6. _ o _ _ a _

7. _ a _ u _ _ a _

8. a u _ u _ _

9. _ a _ u a _ _

10. _ o _ e _ _ e _

11. _ a _ _ _

12. _ u _ e

English Fundamentals Worksheet
Days, Months & Seasons 2

Fill in the gaps to spell the names of days, months and seasons:

1. _ u _ _ a _
2. _ _ _ i _ _
3. _ e _ _ e _ _ a _
4. _ e _ e _ _ e _
5. _ u _ _ e _
6. _ u _ _
7. _ i _ _ e _
8. _ a _
9. _ e _ _ e _ _ e _
10. A u _ u _ _
11. _ u e _ _ a _

English Fundamentals Worksheet
Days of the Week

Tick below to show the correct spellings:

1. a) Sunday b) Sanday c) sunday d) snday

2. a) Manday b) monday c) Monday d) Munday

3. a) Tusday b) tuesday c) Teusday d) Tuesday

4. a) Wensday b) Wednesday c) Wenesday d) wednesday

5. a) Thursday b) Tuesday c) Thorsday d) thurday

6. a) friday b) Friday c) Frieday d) feriday

7. a) Soturday b) Saturda c) saterday d) Saturday

English Fundamentals Worksheet
Months of the Year

Tick below to show the correct spellings:

1. a) Janary b) January c) january d) jaNuary

2. a) February b) Febuary c) Feburary d) february

3. a) march b) Marsh c) March d) Marche

4. a) April b) april c) Appril d) Aprl

5. a) may b) Maye c) My d) May

6. a) Jun b) June c) jun d) june

7. a) Julie b) Juli c) July d) july

8. a) August b) Augst c) Argust d) august

9. a) septembre b) September c) Septemper d) Setember

10. a) october b) Octobar c) August d) October

11. a) Novemer b) November c) novembrer d) Novembre

12. a) decembar b) Decembar c) Desember d) December

English Fundamentals Worksheet
Dates 1

Write the full version of the following dates:
Example: 10/08/92   10th August 1992

1. 01/01/97   _____

2. 5 Jun 83   _____

3. 10.07.02   _____

4. 14/08/12   _____

5. 22 Nov 01   _____

6. 31/12/03   _____

7. 3 Feb 90   _____

8. 17.01.00   _____

9. 27/03/95   _____

10. 20 Apr 09   _____

11. 30 Oct '01   _____

12. 9 Jun '11   _____

13. 13/09/02   _____

14. 2 Nov 93   _____

15. 01.01.2000   _____

English Fundamentals Worksheet
Dates 2

Write the full version of the following dates:
Example: 03/06/2013   The 3rd of June 2013

1.   2 Jan 99 _____

2.   Feb 1 '03 _____

3.   Sept 16 '97 _____

4.   02.03.05 _____

5.   1 Mar '04 _____

6.   Aug 04 '11 _____

7.   10.02.96 _____

8.   15.12.2001 _____

9.   29 Oct '02 _____

10. 2. 2. 96 _____

11. 14.5.12 _____

12. May 1 '01 _____

13. 12/11/98 _____

14. Jan 15 '95 _____

15. 4.8.10 _____

Test Your Grammar Skills
Irregular Verbs 1

Complete the verb tables using ***present simple*** *tense:*

To be

I _____

You _____

He _____

She _____

It _____

We _____

They _____

To go

I _____

You _____

He _____

She _____

It _____

We _____

They _____

To do

I _____

You _____

He _____

She _____

It _____

We _____

They _____

To have

I _____

You _____

He _____

She _____

It _____

We _____

They _____

Test Your Grammar Skills
Irregular Verbs 2

*Complete the verb tables using **past simple** tense:*

To be

I _____

You _____

He _____

She _____

It _____

We _____

They _____

To go

I _____

You _____

He _____

She _____

It _____

We _____

They _____

To do

I _____

You _____

He _____

She _____

It _____

We _____

They _____

To have

I _____

You _____

He _____

She _____

It _____

We _____

They _____

Test Your Grammar Skills
Irregular Verbs 3

Complete the verb tables using **present continuous** *tense:*

To be

I _____

You _____

He _____

She _____

It _____

We _____

They _____

To go

I _____

You _____

He _____

She _____

It _____

We _____

They _____

To do

I _____

You _____

He _____

She _____

It _____

We _____

They _____

To have

I _____

You _____

He _____

She _____

It _____

We _____

They _____

Test Your Grammar Skills
Capital Letters 1

Tick the words that should start with a capital letter, then write them out correctly:

nice	trousers
john	quickly
school	january
get	come
england	sarah
pizza	student
pizza hut	king edward high school
single	atlantic ocean
coconut	fridge
chair	butter
monday	december
new york	french

Test Your Grammar Skills
Capital Letters 2

Tick the words that should start with a capital letter, then write them out correctly:

dress	good
like	easily
hospital	august
claire	steven
spain	went
tomato ketchup	doctor
five	doctor i p jones
washing machine	orange
mount everest	burger king
cupboard	wait
indian	manchester general hospital
paris	wednesday

Test Your Grammar Skills
Sentence Punctuation 1

Write the sentences and add capital letters, full stops and question marks:

1. my sister's name is jackie

_____

2. friday is my favourite day of the week

_____

3. i like watching eastenders on bbc 1

_____

4. charles dickens was a famous writer he was born in portsmouth

_____

5. lisa and chantal are going on holiday to portugal in may

_____

6. did you go to school today

_____

7. my new address is 248 normanton road in nottingham

_____

8. when are you going to the hospital

_____

9. my doctor is getting a new receptionist she's called louise robson

_____

10. ben and i are going to look round leicester grammar school on wednesday

_____

Test Your Grammar Skills
Sentence Punctuation 2

Write the sentences and add capital letters, full stops and question marks:

1. how do I get to the library from here

_____

2. the coach for london leaves in about half an hour

_____

3. my birthday is in september i usually go out for a drink with my friends

_____

4. what do you want for dinner tonight

_____

5. birmingham is the second largest city in the uk

_____

6. i'll have a coke please and two packets of walkers crisps

_____

7. if you need to see a consultant go to the derbyshire royal infirmary

_____

8. mary poppins is my mum's favourite film she likes julie andrews

_____

9. i drive a red fiat punto and my uncle drives a green bmw

_____

10. i joined morton park golf club last week it was very expensive

_____

Test Your Grammar Skills
To Be Questions
(Present Simple) 1

Rearrange the words in each sentence to make a question using verb 'to be' in the present simple tense. Don't forget to put a capital letter at the start of each sentence and a question mark at the end:

1. what brother's is name your

   _____

2. is what address your

   _____

3. favourite is your food what

   _____

4. is your what name

   _____

5. date the what today is

   _____

6. much how that shirt is

   _____

7. are how you

   _____

8. your what is surname

   _____

9. your postcode what is

   _____

10. your when birthday is

   _____

To Be Questions
(Present Simple) 2

Rearrange the words in each sentence to make a question using verb 'to be' in the present simple tense. Don't forget to put a capital letter at the start of each sentence and a question mark at the end:

1. are toilets where the

   _____

2. you where from are

   _____

3. phone is what your number

   _____

4. the answer what is

   _____

5. your what nationality is

   _____

6. is it old how

   _____

7. your best who is friend

   _____

8. one which it is

   _____

9. my shirt where is

   _____

10. old how you are

   _____

To Be Questions
(Present Simple) 3

Rearrange the words in each sentence to make a question using verb 'to be' in the present simple tense. Don't forget to put a capital letter at the start of each sentence and a question mark at the end:

1. is your what name first

   _____

2. capital Australia the what is of

   _____

3. is that car friend's your

   _____

4. outside it is cold

   _____

5. when the concert is

   _____

6. his parents are nice

   _____

7. how there your many are class people in

   _____

8. your what is favourite colour

   _____

9. was Battle of when the Hastings

   _____

10. you are OK

   _____

Test Your Grammar Skills

To Do Questions
(Present Simple) 1

Rearrange the words in each sentence to make a question using verb 'to do' as an auxiliary verb in the present simple tense. Don't forget to put a capital letter at the start of each sentence and a question mark at the end:

1. free do in time do you your what

    _____

2. where you do live

    _____

3. do you how do

    _____

4. how you there get do

    _____

5. do what you living for do a

    _____

6. you what think do

    _____

7. what want you do

    _____

8. want who to you do to speak

    _____

9. where do to go you want

    _____

10. do you him know

    _____

Test Your Grammar Skills

To Do Questions
(Present Simple) 2

Rearrange the words in each sentence to make a question using verb 'to do' as an auxiliary verb in the present simple tense. Don't forget to put a capital letter at the start of each sentence and a question mark at the end:

1. you do to have ask

   _____

2. want lunch when to do you have

   _____

3. do you stamps have any

   _____

4. do have you brothers any and sisters

   _____

5. do work you where

   _____

6. what want do you breakfast for

   _____

7. do who you are think you

   _____

8. newspapers which you do read

   _____

9. why you like do playing snooker

   _____

10. you do and want fish chips some

   _____

Test Your Grammar Skills

To Do Questions

(Present Simple) 3

Rearrange the words in each sentence to make a question using verb 'to do' as an auxiliary verb in the present simple tense. Don't forget to put a capital letter at the start of each sentence and a question mark at the end:

1. where come do you from

    _____

2. English do think boring you is

    _____

3. one best do which like you

    _____

4. what want do they know to

    _____

5. you do OK feel

    _____

6. watching does enjoy she films old

    _____

7. hard does Louis work

    _____

8. do want you start to course this

    _____

9. you do library the know to way the

    _____

10. do want come with you me to you

    _____

Test Your Grammar Skills
To Have Questions
(Present Perfect) 1

Rearrange the words in each sentence to make a question using verb 'to have' as an auxiliary verb in the present perfect tense. Don't forget to put a capital letter at the start of each sentence and a question mark at the end:

1. where you have been

    _____

2. what been have doing you

    _____

3. have you why come class this to

    _____

4. when to got have arrive I

    _____

5. money have you any got

    _____

6. the time got have you please

    _____

7. have my you friend seen

    _____

8. looked have every you in cupboard

    _____

9. closed curtains the have you

    _____

10. she why hasn't the washing done up

    _____

Test Your Grammar Skills
To Have Questions
(Present Perfect) 2

Rearrange the words in each sentence to make a question using verb 'to have' as an auxiliary verb in the present perfect tense. Don't forget to put a capital letter at the start of each sentence and a question mark at the end:

1. you here have before been

   _____

2. which you films seen have

   _____

3. any oranges got have you

   _____

4. have had you your tea

   _____

5. finished have you magazine that with

   _____

6. I'm leaving has he told you that

   _____

7. you have got yet your certificate

   _____

8. changed have you phone number your

   _____

9. have what you today learnt

   _____

10. have you bought birthday a for Jane card

    _____

Test Your Grammar Skills
To Have Questions
(Present Perfect) 3

Rearrange the words in each sentence to make a question using verb 'to have' as an auxiliary verb in the present perfect tense. Don't forget to put a capital letter at the start of each sentence and a question mark at the end:

1. when you got to have go

    _____

2. he why hasn't painting finished bathroom the

    _____

3. finished have your meal you

    _____

4. heard you the new CD Bon Jovi have by

    _____

5. what saying have to been they you

    _____

6. what hair you your have done to

    _____

7. photos has he done what my with

    _____

8. holiday where have been on they

    _____

9. she who has talking been to

    _____

10. haven't why tidied you up

    _____

English Fundamentals Worksheet
Homophones 1

Homophones are words that sound the same as each other, but have different spellings and meanings. Put together the words that sound the same:

board	mail	by
dear	heel	its
bare	knows	for
be	find	high
aren't	mourning	meet

1. fined _____
2. nose _____
3. bee _____
4. it's _____
5. male _____
6. bored _____
7. morning _____
8. buy _____
9. hi _____
10. bear _____
11. meat _____
12. deer _____
13. four _____
14. heal _____
15. aunt _____

English Fundamentals Worksheet
Homophones 2

Homophones are words that sound the same as each other, but have different spellings and meanings. Put together the words that sound the same:

piece	pear	one
loan	new	or
plane	read	pail
poor	no	raise
mind	none	night

1. pale _____

2. won _____

3. mined _____

4. know _____

5. lone _____

6. pair _____

7. plain _____

8. knew _____

9. red _____

10. pour _____

11. peace _____

12. knight _____

13. nun _____

14. rays _____

15. oar _____

Part Two

English Fundamentals Worksheet

Numbers 1

Write the answers to the following sums in words:

+ plus	- minus	x multiplied by
	+ divided by	= equals

1. four plus ten equals   _____

2. twenty five plus three plus fourteen equals _____

3. nine minus seven equals   _____

4. thirty two minus seventeen equals   _____

5. seven plus one minus five equals   _____

6. ten multiplied by eight equals   _____

7. four multiplied by fifteen equals   _____

8. thirty two divided by eight equals   _____

9. sixty divided by ten equals   _____

10. one hundred and twenty divided by four equals _____

11. seven multiplied by three plus sixteen equals _____

12. eighteen minus nine plus forty four equals _____

English Fundamentals Worksheet

Numbers 2

Write the answers to the following sums in words:

+ plus   **- minus**   **x multiplied by**

+ divided by   **= equals**

1. five plus eleven equals _____

2. sixteen plus nineteen plus eight equals _____

3. forty five minus seven equals _____

4. twenty two minus thirty one equals _____

5. thirty seven plus four minus six equals _____

6. twenty nine multiplied by five equals _____

7. three multiplied by sixteen equals _____

8. fifty five divided by five equals _____

9. ninety divided by six equals _____

10. one thousand one hundred divided by four equals _____

11. forty multiplied by two plus four equals _____

12. fifteen minus eight plus sixty equals _____

English Fundamentals Worksheet

Numbers 3

Complete the sums below, writing your answers in words:

a) **ten plus two equals** _____

    add fifteen _____

    add forty one _____

    subtract five _____

    multiply by three _____

b) **nineteen minus seven equals** _____

    subtract four _____

    multiply by five _____

    add seventeen _____

    subtract fifteen _____

c) **forty multiplied by two equals** _____

    add eighteen _____

    add fifty eight _____

    subtract ten _____

    multiply by four _____

English Fundamentals Worksheet

Numbers 4

Complete the sums below, writing your answers in words:

a)   **fifteen minus three equals**   _____

     add eight   _____

     subtract one   _____

     multiply by nine   _____

     add seven   _____

b)   **fifty one plus four equals**   _____

     subtract thirty   _____

     multiply by three   _____

     subtract eighteen   _____

     add twelve   _____

c)   **eighty two minus six equals**   _____

     add sixty three   _____

     subtract twenty nine   _____

     add ten   _____

     multiply by four   _____

English Fundamentals Worksheet

Numbers 5

Complete the sums below, writing your answers in words:

a) **one plus fifteen equals**

  _____

  add twenty one

  _____

  add thirty five

  _____

  subtract eight

  _____

  multiply by ten

  _____

b) **seventy two minus one equals**

  _____

  subtract six

  _____

  subtract twelve

  _____

  multiply by four

  _____

  add two thousand one hundred and
  six

  _____

c) **one thousand and fifty plus
  ninety nine equals**

  _____

  add four

  _____

  subtract eighty one

  _____

  multiply by two

  _____

  add four thousand five hundred
  and seventy five

  _____

English Fundamentals Worksheet

Prices 1

Write the answers to these sums in words.
Example: £2.99 + £4.60 = seven pounds fifty nine pence

1.   £3.50 + £2.99 =   _____

2.   £10.20 + £4.99 =   _____

3.   £4.68 + £9.99 =   _____

4.   £20.50 + 17.35 =   _____

5.   £1.99 + £6.89 =   _____

6.   £103.01 + £243.50 =   _____

7.   £10 - £3.50 =   _____

8.   £25.50 - £12 =   _____

9.   £7.99 - £3.50 =   _____

10. £13.80 - £4.04 =   _____

11. £28 + £15.50 - 79p =   _____

12. £10 + £12 + £14.40 - 29p = _____

English Fundamentals Worksheet

Prices 2

Write the answers to these sums in words:
Example: £4.99 + £9.50 = fourteen pounds forty nine pence

1. £2.85 + £3.95 = _____

2. £17.69 + £4.80 = _____

3. £2.99 x 3 = _____

4. £4.50 x 4 = _____

5. £35 + £2.99 + £4.99 = _____

6. 80p - 55p = _____

7. £7.95 + £18.50 = _____

8. £1.50 - 23p = _____

9. 95p + £10.48 = _____

10. £110.99 + £12.99 + £4.99 = _____

11. 89p - 22p = _____

12. 68p + £2.89 - £2.50 = _____

English Fundamentals Worksheet

Ordinals 1
Months of the Year

Complete the sentences using one of these ordinals:

first	fourth	seventh	tenth
second	fifth	eighth	eleventh
third	sixth	ninth	twelfth

1. October is the _____ month of the year.

2. January is the _____ month of the year.

3. April is the _____ month of the year.

4. March is the _____ month of the year.

5. September is the _____ month of the year.

6. June is the _____ month of the year.

7. May is the _____ month of the year.

8. February is the _____ month of the year.

9. December is the _____ month of the year.

10. July is the _____ month of the year.

11. November is the _____ month of the year.

12. August is the _____ month of the year.

English Fundamentals Worksheet
Ordinals 2
The Alphabet

Complete the sentences using an ordinal, for example, 'first', 'second', etc.

1.   **A**   is the _____ letter of the alphabet.

2.   **P**   is the _____ letter of the alphabet.

3.   **E**   is the _____ letter of the alphabet.

4.   **X**   is the _____ letter of the alphabet.

5.   **L**   is the _____ letter of the alphabet.

6.   **T**   is the _____ letter of the alphabet.

7.   **O**   is the _____ letter of the alphabet.

8.   **M**   is the _____ letter of the alphabet.

9.   **F**   is the _____ letter of the alphabet.

10.   **G**   is the _____ letter of the alphabet.

11.   **K**   is the _____ letter of the alphabet.

12.   **R**   is the _____ letter of the alphabet.

13.   **U**   is the _____ letter of the alphabet.

14.   **D**   is the _____ letter of the alphabet.

15.   **J**   is the _____ letter of the alphabet.

Test Your Grammar Skills
Opposite Adjectives 1

Match the adjective on the left with its opposite adjective on the right:

clever	high
poor	soft
sunny	stupid
wet	rich
long	rainy
fat	dry
big	short
good	small
hard	thin
low	bad

Test Your Grammar Skills
Opposite Adjectives 2

Match the adjective on the left with its opposite adjective on the right:

light	narrow
warm	short
old	cool
odd	young
fast	flat
expensive	normal
hungry	cheap
uneven	full
wide	slow
tall	dark

Test Your Grammar Skills
Comparatives & Superlatives 1

Write the appropriate comparative and superlative form of these adjectives:

adjective	comparative	superlative
example: big	bigger	biggest
1. light	_____	_____
2. clever	_____	_____
3. sunny	_____	_____
4. hard	_____	_____
5. thin	_____	_____
6. good	_____	_____
7. poor	_____	_____
8. short	_____	_____
9. late	_____	_____
10. happy	_____	_____

Test Your Grammar Skills
Comparatives & Superlatives 2

Write the appropriate comparative and superlative form of these adjectives:

adjective	comparative	superlative
example:		
big	bigger	biggest
1. shady	_____	_____
2. stupid	_____	_____
3. rainy	_____	_____
4. soft	_____	_____
5. fat	_____	_____
6. bad	_____	_____
7. rich	_____	_____
8. long	_____	_____
9. early	_____	_____
10. sad	_____	_____

Test Your Grammar Skills
Comparatives & Superlatives 3

Write the appropriate comparative and superlative form of these adjectives:

	adjective	comparative	superlative
	example:		
	big	bigger	biggest
1.	nice	_____	_____
2.	cold	_____	_____
3.	clean	_____	_____
4.	young	_____	_____
5.	fast	_____	_____
6.	large	_____	_____
7.	hungry	_____	_____
8.	narrow	_____	_____
9.	red	_____	_____
10.	near	_____	_____

Test Your Grammar Skills
Comparatives & Superlatives 4

Write the appropriate comparative and superlative form of these adjectives:

	adjective	comparative	superlative
	example: big	bigger	biggest
1.	nasty	_____	_____
2.	hot	_____	_____
3.	dirty	_____	_____
4.	old	_____	_____
5.	slow	_____	_____
6.	small	_____	_____
7.	full	_____	_____
8.	wide	_____	_____
9.	green	_____	_____
10.	far	_____	_____

Test Your Grammar Skills
Indefinite Articles 1

Which indefinite article should we write in front of the following words -

'a' or 'an'?

1. _____ chair

2. _____ girl

3. _____ school

4. _____ egg

5. _____ hour

6. _____ apple

7. _____ exam

8. _____ hospital

9. _____ year

10. _____ university

11. _____ address

12. _____ ear

13. _____ sheep

14. _____ tie

15. _____ union

Test Your Grammar Skills
Indefinite Articles 2

Which indefinite article should we write in front of the following words -
'a' or 'an'?

1._____ orange

2._____ ice cream

3._____ pencil

4._____ umbrella

5._____ shoe

6._____ number

7._____ heater

8._____ interview

9._____ application form

10._____ heir

11._____ computer

12._____ bag

13._____ octopus

14._____ ewe

15._____ fridge

Test Your Grammar Skills
Countable & Uncountable Nouns 1

Complete the sentences using either **'a'** *or* **'some'**:

There is _____ sand in my shoe.

There is _____ five pound note in my wallet.

There is _____ wine in the cupboard.

There is _____ butter in the fridge.

There is _____ peanut butter on the worktop.

There is _____ radio in the kitchen.

There is _____ toothbrush in the bathroom.

There is _____ jam in the cupboard.

There is _____ magazine in the living room

There is _____ queue at the post office.

There is _____ luggage in the car.

There is _____ suitcase in the bedroom.

There is _____ flour in the cupboard.

There is _____ sugar in your tea.

There is _____ bicycle outside.

Test Your Grammar Skills
Countable & Uncountable Nouns 2

Complete the sentences using either **'a'** *or* **'some'**:

There is _____ rice in the cupboard.

There is _____ dog in the garden.

There is _____ postman coming to the door.

There is _____ alcohol in the fridge.

There is _____ bathroom upstairs.

There is _____ computer in the office.

There is _____ oil on the floor.

There is _____ ice on the windscreen.

There is _____ shirt in the tumble dryer.

There is _____ homework to do later on.

There is _____ food on the table.

There is _____ cheese in the fridge.

There is _____ light switch on the wall.

There is _____ vinegar on your chips.

There is _____ pen in my pocket.

English Fundamentals Worksheet
Uncountable Nouns

advice	furniture	money	shopping
air	gold	music	silver
alcohol	grass	news	snow
art	ground	noise	space
beef	happiness	oil	speed
blood	history	oxygen	steam
butter	homework	paper	sugar
cheese	honey	patience	sunshine
chewing	hope	pay	tea
gum	ice	peace	tennis
chocolate	information	peanut	time
coffee	jam	butter	toothpaste
confusion	juice	pepper	traffic
cotton	knowledge	petrol	trousers
education	lamb	plastic	vinegar
electricity	lightning	pork	washing up
entertainment	literature	power	washing up liquid
experience	love	pressure	water
fiction	luck	rain	weather
flour	luggage	rice	wine
food	meat	sadness	wood
forgiveness	milk	salt	wool
fresh air	mist	sand	work

Part Three

Test Your Grammar Skills

There are & There is

Write ten sentences using the words in the table.

there is	a	people	in the	hall
		cupboards magazines		lounge
		bath		dining room
		bed		office
	an	sink		spare room
there are		armchair		garden
		umbrella		loft
	some	dining table		conservatory
		knives and forks		kitchen
		plant		bedroom
				bathroom
				airing cupboard

Test Your Grammar Skills
Personal Pronouns 1

Fill in the gaps using either 'I' or 'me':

1. Give that book to _____.

2. _____ don't like working in shops.

3. Does your friend know_____?

4. _____ and Ted are going out for lunch.

5. _____ need to ask you something.

6. _____'m a vegetarian.

7. _____ was the first one to finish my exam.

8. This is a picture of _____ and mum on holiday.

9. This is the house they showed _____ .

10. Did you know that _____ live in Manchester?

11. Jenny told _____ that you went to London last week.

12. _____ will see you soon.

13. Deepak is older than _____ .

14. Call _____ when you get there.

15. This is the house where _____ was born.

Test Your Grammar Skills
Personal Pronouns 2

*Fill in the gaps using either **'he'** or **'him'**:*

1. _____always goes home early on Tuesdays.

2. I asked _____ for some help.

3. _____ asked, "What's her problem?"

4. _____ was always a bit quiet.

5. That's easy for_____ to say.

6. Do you want to see _____ now?

7. _____ needs a new pair of shoes.

8. I think that _____ is really selfish.

9. Can you ask_____ ?

10. _____ wasn't very well last week.

11. _____ put on his coat and went out.

12. Gillian gave the largest piece of cake to _____ .

13. I love spending time with _____ .

14. Everyone told_____ to be quiet.

15. There's something strange about _____ .

Test Your Grammar Skills
Personal Pronouns 3

*Fill in the gaps using either **'she'** or **'her'**:*

1. _____ thought he was joking.

2._____ has got long hair.

3. I see_____ on the bus every day.

4. John called _____ at half past nine.

5. Sally's sister gave _____ a new jacket.

6. I know _____ studies English.

7. _____ 's quite serious, isn't she?

8. _____ 's not interested in geography.

9. That guitar belongs to _____ .

10. Is _____ going on holiday with you?

11. _____ waited in the rain for half an hour.

12. I told _____ that you can't meet _____ .

13._____ picked up the bag.

14. My neighbour said that _____ wasn't coming.

15. Ask my sister if _____ saw him.

Test Your Grammar Skills
Personal Pronouns 4

Fill in the gaps using either 'we' or 'us':

1. _____ aren't interested.

2. Nobody told _____ .

3. They don't believe _____ .

4. Will_____ be able to meet up?

5. This is what _____ wanted.

6. They saw _____ walking down the road.

7. _____ agree with you.

8. Tell _____ what you mean.

9. _____ hope that you enjoy yourselves.

10. Can _____ tell you tomorrow?

11. _____ don't want to go out.

12. This puts _____ in a difficult position.

13. That's impossible for _____ .

14. _____ 'll do what _____ can.

15. Thank you for inviting _____ .

Test Your Grammar Skills
Personal Pronouns 5

*Fill in the gaps using either **'they'** or **'them'**:*

1. I don't know _____ at all.

2. _____ can't hear you.

3. Ask _____ yourself.

4. Who is that man with _____ ?

5. _____ went to the cinema with Linda and Rachael last night.

6. Please tell _____ that _____ are early.

7. Somebody wants to see _____ .

8. I will put _____ on the waiting list.

9. _____ are at the football match.

10. Did _____ see you there?

11. I've never heard of _____ .

12. I want to invite _____ , but I think _____ are busy.

13. _____ cut the grass, just like I asked _____ to.

14. It was kind of _____ to say _____ would help.

15. What colour curtains do _____ want?

Test Your Grammar Skills
Personal Pronouns 6

Subject pronouns	I	you	he	she	it	we	they
Object pronouns	me	you	him	her	it	us	them

Fill in each gap with either a subject pronoun or object pronoun:

1. Have you seen my dad? _____'s wearing a red shirt.

2. Are_____ going to finish your dinner?

3. I don't like Christopher. _____ really annoys_____.

4. Your bag is over there. Take_____ with_____ when you go.

5. We always go to bed early. Ten o'clock is late for_____.

6. Her shoes were dirty, so _____cleaned _____ .

7. I'm going to the cinema. Do _____ want to come with_____?

8. My brother rang last night._____ was great to talk to_____.

9. Emily saw _____at the restaurant. They were having lunch.

10. The boy came up to_____ and took my hand.

Test Your Grammar Skills
Personal Pronouns 7

Subject pronouns	I	you	he	she	it	we	they
Object pronouns	me	you	him	her	it	us	them

Fill in each gap with either a subject pronoun or object pronoun:

1. I don't think the shop is open._____ usually closes at five thirty.

2. I showed_____ my photos. He thought_____were boring.

3. "How much is that CD?" "_____think_____'s £11.99."

4. Ben isn't coming to see the film._____'s seen_____already.

5. It's sunny today, isn't_____?

6. I went to see my aunt._____ was pleased to see_____.

7. It's good to see_____ all. Thanks for coming.

8. Lara's boyfriend has broken up with _____. _____told_____that _____doesn't love her any more.

9. _____were annoyed when their meal was late.

10. Adele said goodbye to her brother. She was sad to watch_____ go.

Test Your Grammar Skills
Adverbs of Frequency 1

Complete the graph by adding these words,
along with a percentage to show frequency:

seldom

often

occasionally

don't usually

usually

hardly

ever

sometimes

frequently

100%   **always**

0%   **never**

Test Your Grammar Skills
Adverbs of Frequency 2

Write ten sentences that are true for you, using adverbs of frequency.
Then write ten sentences about your friend
*(use **he** or **she** and change the verb form):*

	always	have lunch with Tony Blair.
	usually	use public transport.
	frequently	go to the theatre.
	often	smoke twenty cigarettes a day.
I	sometimes	phone directory enquiries.
	don't usually	wash my hands before meals.
	seldom	have a pint after work.
	occasionally	put vinegar on my chips.
	hardly ever	look for a job at the Jobcentre.
	never	play football at the weekend.

Test Your Grammar Skills
Adverbs of Frequency 3

Write ten sentences that are true for you, using adverbs of frequency.
Then write ten sentences about your friend
(use he *or* she *and change the verb form):*

	always	go shopping on a Monday afternoon.
	usually	watch TV in the evenings.
	frequently	go out to see a concert.
	often	wake up at six o'clock in the morning.
I	sometimes	arrive at work on time.
	don't usually	have lunch in a posh restaurant.
	seldom	brush my teeth before going to bed.
	occasionally	have a bath or shower every day.
	hardly ever	have a cup of tea when I first wake up.
	never	listen to BBC Radio 4.

Test Your Grammar Skills
First Conditional 1

If I feel tired,	I'll go to bed.
If I can't afford a new watch,	I won't buy one.
If I see Carla,	I'll tell you.
If you are going out,	let me know.
If you're hungry,	you can have an apple.
If I'm going to be late,	I'll give you a call.
If I need a new suit,	I'll have to buy one.
If I get a pay rise,	we can go on holiday.
If you bring your car over,	I might clean it for you.
If the bus is early,	I will miss it.
If it starts raining,	I'm going to get wet.
If my brother is there,	he'll look after you.
If that sale is on,	I might get some bargains.
If the CD stops,	press 'play' to start it again.
If the doctor thinks it's necessary,	I'll have to have an operation.

Test Your Grammar Skills
First Conditional 2

If the tiger starts growling,	move away as quietly as you can.
If you damage my car,	I'll be really annoyed.
If I give you ten pounds,	can you do some shopping for me?
If you think I'm joking,	I'll show you that I'm serious.
If anyone knows,	Sarah will.
If you don't like dogs,	you won't like Lee's new puppies.
If Leanne is going,	I might go as well.
If you study hard,	you'll get a certificate.
If tomorrow is fine,	we could go to the beach.
If I wear a coat,	I won't get cold.
If my sister phones,	you should speak to her.
If you want to go swimming later,	pack your swimming things.
If you've finished with the newspaper,	give it to me.
If you don't know the right spelling,	look it up in a dictionary.
If the tap continues to leak,	you should call a plumber.

Test Your Grammar Skills
Wh Questions 1

*Complete each sentence, using **what**, **where**, **when**, **who** or **why**:*

what (information)
where (location)
when (time)
who (people)
why (reasons)

1. _____'s the time please?

2. _____ did I just say?

3. _____ do you think you are?

4. _____ is my coat?

5. _____ do you want to leave? This evening?

6. _____ didn't you go to college this morning?

7. _____ was the Battle of Hastings?

8. _____ are you looking for?

9. _____'s your name?

10. _____ is the front door open?

11. _____ is the star of 'Spiderman'?

12. _____ didn't you call me last night?

13. _____ do you live?

14. _____ did you go to last night?

15. "_____ did you leave school?" "In 2010."

Test Your Grammar Skills
Wh Questions 2

*Complete each sentence, using **what**, **where**, **when**, **who** or **why**:*

what (information)
where (location)
when (time)
who (people)
why (reasons)

1. _____ do you work?

2. _____ were you talking to yesterday?

3. _____ 's going on?

4. _____ are you still in bed at four in the afternoon?

5. _____ is your birthday?

6. _____ did the builders get here?

7. _____ did you put my magazine?

8. _____ is the oldest person in this room?

9. _____ are you going to tidy up your room?

10. _____ is there a scratch on my new car?

11. _____ is your sister's occupation?

12. _____ should I talk to about my wages?

13. _____ 's your favourite food?

14. _____ has your friend been?

15. _____ did the chicken cross the road?

Test Your Grammar Skills
Compound Nouns 1

Compound nouns are formed from two or more other nouns, for example:

break + fast = breakfast

*Can you match the words on the **left** with the words on the **right** to make fourteen compound nouns?*

after	day
birth	work
book	time
table	port
air	hood
tea	noon
pan	top
paper	shelf
cave	back
horse	cake
parent	board
home	man
car	pet
cup	fly

Test Your Grammar Skills
Compound Nouns 2

Compound nouns are formed from two or more other nouns, for example:

break + fast = breakfast

*Can you match the words on the **left** with the words on the **right** to make fourteen compound nouns?*

time	side
bath	house
in	out
out	hanger
no	table
cliff	eater
police	body
some	fall
bread	room
ant	bin
water	break
wheel	woman
fall	barrow
day	times

Test Your Grammar Skills
Compound Nouns 3

Compound nouns are formed from two or more other nouns, for example:

break + fast = breakfast

*Can you match the words on the **left** with the words on the **right** to make fourteen compound nouns?*

lamp	valid
wheel	shade
foot	chair
in	ball
human	man
shop	age
fire	lifter
foot	bike
motor	suit
butter	sake
rail	fly
mini	way
name	skirt
track	kind

Test Your Grammar Skills
Daily Routines 1

A) Complete the sentences below using a present simple verb:

I _____ the newspaper at 8.00am.

I _____ a coffee break at 10.30am.

I _____ a shower at 7.30am.

I _____ lunch at 1.00pm.

I _____ a bus to work at 8.30am.

I _____ up at 7.15am.

I _____ work at 9.00am.

I _____ breakfast at 7.45am.

I _____ up at 7.05am.

B) Write the sentences in the order that they happen.

*C) Next: write about **your** daily routine.*

Test Your Grammar Skills
Daily Routines 2

A) Complete the sentences below using a present simple verb:

I _____ to my friend on the phone at 2.30pm.

I_____ an email at 2.40pm.

I _____home at 5.00pm.

I _____my guitar at 9.00pm.

I _____ dinner at 6.00pm.

I _____to bed at 11.10pm.

I _____football at 7.00pm.

I _____a book at 10.00pm.

I_____to the radio at 10.40pm.

I _____TV at 8.30pm.

I _____the dishes at 6.30pm.

I _____to sleep at about 11.20pm.

B) Write the sentences in the order that they happen.

*C) Next: write about **your** daily routine.*

Test Your Grammar Skills
Complete the Sentences 1

Write the sentences and complete them by choosing the best option below:

1. I live in a_____
a) car. b) office. c) house. d) factory.

2. I like watching TV every_____
a) year. b) minute. c) night. d) fortnight.

3. I like wearing_____
a) curtains. b) jeans. c) newspapers. d) a box.

4. In the summer it is _____
a) interesting. b) dark. c) expensive. d) hot.

5. In my living room I have a_____
a) bed. b) bath. c) garden chair. d) sofa.

6. I like my job because it is _____
a) enjoyable. b) terrible. c) boring. d) dull.

7. My favourite meal is_____
a) coffee.   b) milk c) water. d) sausage and chips.

8. Last night I saw a film at the_____
a) Indian restaurant. b) cinema. c) school. d) gym.

9. I have a girlfriend called_____
a) Terry. b) Bob. c) Laura. d) Jeff.

10. I work in a_____
a) shop. b) phone booth. c) lift. d) optician's.

Test Your Grammar Skills
Complete the Sentences 2

Write the sentences and complete them by choosing the best option below:

1. My dad is a_____

a) fireman. b) fireplace. c) fire brigade. d) fire engine.

2. I don't like taking _____

a) exam. b) exam paper. c) exams. d) exam preparation.

3. When do you want to go _____

a) homework? b) home? c) house? d) walk?

4. How much is a _____

a) price? b) tickets? c) ticket? d) pay?

5. My sister is twelve years _____

a) older. b) old. c) young. d) aged.

6. These questions are_____

a) easier. b) hardest. c) easy. d) easiest.

7. That clock on the wall is _____

a) young.   b) fast. c) heavy. d) slowed.

8. Are you coming home _____

a) yesterday? b) tomorrow? c) last week? d) a week ago?

9. I go shopping twice a _____

a) hour. b) week. c) sometimes. d) never.

10. On Friday night I go to the _____

a) pubs. b) visit. c) cafes. d) pub.

Test Your Grammar Skills
Complete the Sentences 3

Write the sentences and complete them by choosing the best option below:

1. How do I get to the post office from_____

a) everywhere? b) left? c) here? d) there?

2. I wish I could go on_____

a) break. b) weekend away. c) holiday. d) travelling.

3. There's something wrong with the_____

a) cleaned. b) dust. c) hoovered. d) dishwasher.

4. Friday is my favourite day of the_____

a) month. b) week. c) afternoon. d) year.

5. I start my new job next _____

a) monthly. b) month's time. c) months. d) month.

6. The film was really_____

a) badly. b) good. c) lonely. d) especially.

7. My exam results are _____

a) glad. b) surprised. c) disappointing. d) pleased.

8. The coach is waiting for_____

a) some. b) us. c) student. d) driver.

9. Nobody knows where the book _____

a) gone. b) said. c) were. d) is.

10. I like listening to the_____

a) cupboard. b) heater. c) radio. d) pictures.

Test Your Grammar Skills
Complete the Sentences 4

Write the sentences and complete them by choosing the best option below:

1. I'm taking my wife to see a_____

a) theatre. b) play. c) poster. d) screen.

2. In the winter we leave the heating_____

a) under. b) in. c) on. d) near.

3. A giraffe has got a long_____

a) head. b) neck. c) arms. d) shoulder.

4. Can you pass me my folder_____

a) thanks? b) please? c) excuse me? d) hi?

5. I washed my hair this_____

a) later. b) never. c) morning. d) time.

6. Hussain can't play the_____

a) lamp. b) football. c) guitarist. d) piano.

7. My boss was really _____

a) pink. b) busy. c) entertain. d) into.

8. It's her birthday on the_____

a) fiftieth. b) day. c) eleventh. d) fourteen.

9. The concert started on _____

a) hour. b) arrived. c) time. d) month.

10. Her sink is blocked. She needs a _____

a) baker. b) dentist. c) plumber. d) doctor.

Test Your Grammar Skills
Complete the Sentences 5

Write the sentences and complete them by choosing the best option below:

1. I need to go to the bank before it_____

a) opens. b) pays. c) arrives. d) closes.

2. Spring is my favourite_____

a) month. b) week. c) season. d) fortnight.

3. I'm going to get my hair_____

a) made. b) cut. c) covered. d) on.

4. The Romans came to Britain in_____

a) 45 RPM. b) 7.45 AM. c) 8th May. d) 55 BC.

5. Have we got any more _____

a) sausage? b) baked bean? c) bacon? d) biscuit?

6. What is the capital of _____

a) UK? b) London? c) South America? d) the UK?

7. We've booked our_____

a) travel agent. b) holiday. c) library. d) pizzas.

8. Have you got a student _____

a) with? b) loan? c) line? d) discounts?

9. When will my car be_____

a) ready? b) real? c) relied? d) related?

10. Have you ever met my_____

a) soldier? b) dad's? c) sister? d) famous?

Test Your Grammar Skills
Complete the Sentences 6

Write the sentences and complete them by choosing the best option below:

1. Do you mind if I have a _____

a) washing?   b) watch TV?   c) show?   d) shower?

2. My mother lives in_____

a) a field.   b) Newcastle.   c) wherever.   d) road.

3. Do you like crossword_____.

a) please?   b) puzzles?   c) game?   d) written?

4. What's your sister's _____.

a) neighbour?   b) friends?   c) name?   d) aged?

5. We live in a semi-detached_____

a) bank.   b) garden.   c) estate.   d) house.

6. The only one who knows is _____

a) Harry Miller.   b) cat.   c) the computer.   d) everybody.

7. We aren't going to make _____

a) us.   b) it.   c) in.   d) if.

8. They are just good _____

a) of you.   b) sense.   c) friends.   d) advice.

9. My car won't _____ a

) drive.   b) start.   c) gone.   d) broken.

10. We are saving up to get _____

a) buying.   b) shopping.   c) married.   d) expensive.

Test Your Grammar Skills
Complete the Sentences 7

Write the sentences and complete them by choosing the best option below:

1. This film is really_____

a) good. b) greater. c) open. d) enjoyed.

2. Can I borrow your _____

a) elbow? b) ruler? c) waiter? d) time?

3. That's the last_____.

a) one. b) isn't it? c) times. d) gone.

4. School is the best time of _____

a) his life. b) their lives. c) your life. d) Owen's life.

5. My leg _____

a) ends. b) goes. c) hurts. d) changes.

6. This problem is_____.

a) often. b) grey. c) early. d) serious.

7. When shall I come _____

a) with? b) round? c) under? d) go on?

8. The policeman told me to_____

a) calm down. b) accident. c) cried. d) replied.

9. Jemma stole my_____

a) achieves. b) age. c) make up. d) disliked.

10. The concert starts at_____.

a) one. b) thirteen. c) time. d) in the evening.

Test Your Grammar Skills
Complete the Sentences 8

Write the sentences and complete them by choosing the best option below:

1. How many children have you_____

a) came? b) own? c) got? d) took?

2. My uncle and aunt are_____

a) people. b) divorced. c) mixed. d) into.

3. I love reading a good_____

a) phone call. b) receipt. c) gas bill. d) novel.

4. The future will be_____

a) afraid. b) bright. c) interested. d) waited.

5. Once upon a _____

a) time. b) who. c) story. d) Time.

6. The man left his_____.

a) future. b) in it. c) keys. d) addressed.

7. I bought some flowers at the_____.

a) optician's. b) market. c) carrier bag. d) bakery.

8. Noel watched his brother_____

a) come home. b) came home. c) lived. d) hear.

9. Your dog is so well-_____

a) travelled. b) meant. c) done. d) behaved.

10. I feel tired after that_____.

a) go swimming. b) walk. c) go out. d) exercised.

Test Your Grammar Skills
Complete the Sentences 9

Write the sentences and complete them by choosing the best option below:

1. The only way is_____

a) about. b) in. c) out. d) up.

2. I'm sorry about_____

a) getting. b) that. c) when. d) who.

3. Aren't those fireworks_____

a) smelly? b) excited. c) lovely? d) gone?

4. I didn't like your _____.

a) name. b) address. c) attitude. d) farmer.

5. Petrol is far too_____.

a) near. b) going. c) great. d) expensive.

6. The shock will kill_____.

a) him. b) everything. c) flowers. d) hers.

7. It doesn't rain every_____

a) afternoons. b) day. c) day? d) all the time.

8. The show must go_____

a) if. b) since. c) on. d) up.

9. Blackpool is on the west _____

a) coast. b) sea. c) lake. d) resort.

10. How many stars are there in the_____

a) air? b) evening? c) sky? d) sky.

Test Your Grammar Skills
Complete the Sentences 10

Write the sentences and complete them by choosing the best option below:

1. We never even said_____.

a) hello. b) good afternoon. c) see ya. d) goodbye.

2. My hands were_____.

a) taken. b) clean. c) serious. d) looked.

3. My husband's name is_____.

a) Derek. b) Emma. c) Charlotte. d) father.

4. The piano is too heavy to_____

a) be. b) got. c) advise. d) move.

5. That girl looks _____

a) hurrah. b) ridiculously. c) silly. d) really.

6. Let's try to save the _____

a) travel. b) impossible. c) planet. d) recycle it.

7. That was 20p cheaper in _____

a) this shop. b) that way. c) this piece. d) her own.

8. Can you speak a bit _____.

a) up a bit? b) please? c) more time? d) louder?

9. The coffee is over_____.

a) then. b) there. c) taken. d) where.

10. Then he told us a_____

a) long. b) time. c) place. d) story.

Test Your Grammar Skills
Complete the Sentences 11

Write the sentences and complete them by choosing the best option below:

1. I don't believe _____

a) in. b) if. c) it. d) is.

2. Who wants to go _____

a) first. b) second time? c) that? d) first?

3. It was only a_____

a) agree. b) fun. c) joke. d) good.

4. Give me a_____.

a) egg. b) ring. c) apple. d) ring me.

5. We don't know what to ._____

a) think. b) thought. c) wished. d) did.

6. It was chucking it_____

a) in. b) down. c) with. d) up.

7. Can I help at _____

a) the morning? b) with you? c) all. d) all?

8. My mum sent me a _____

a) shopping. b) present. c) Letter. d) blue.

9. We didn't enjoy_____.

a) camping. b) camped. c) the curtains. d) us.

10. I live in_____

a) bristol. b) Bristol? c) Bristol. d) BristoL.

Test Your Grammar Skills
Sentence Building 1

Write these words in the correct order to make a sentence:

1. dog My to go on diet. needs a

_____

2. went house I night. friend's my to last

_____

3. to seashore. live the I would near like

_____

4. had some I buy would a car. money If I

_____

5. last my Saturday. was birthday It

_____

6. three-bedroomed I live a in house.

_____

7. new to I buy curtains. some need

_____

8. on Spain. I On going to holiday am Monday

_____

Test Your Grammar Skills
Sentence Building 2

Write these words in the correct order to make a sentence:

1. need I for a stamp letter. my

_____

2. me tell the please? time you Can

_____

3. spaghetti like like but pizza. I don't I

_____

4. My is Oliver book favourite by Dickens. Twist

_____

5. Sunday came my to sister us. On scc

_____

6. felt I early. I so to bed went tired

_____

7. party. else Everybody at the was

_____

8. holiday Would like you them? to with on go

_____

Test Your Grammar Skills
The Plays of William Shakespeare

1. Write these words in the right order to make some famous quotations:

a) be, is be, or not the "To question." to that

_____

b) music food be the of "If love, on." play

_____

c) bold." made made drunk hath which hath them "That me

_____

d) here?" hempen we "What swaggering homespuns have

_____

e) thou yet daughter." art blood, "But flesh, my my my

_____

f) lord, thy husband keeper." thy "Thy life, thy is

_____

g) dear more." the "Once unto once more friends, breach,

_____

h) "A   kingdom My horse!" horse! A a horse! for

_____

2. Write the name of the play, and the character's name.

3. Write the numbers of the Act and Scene where you can find these lines.

Part Four

Test Your Grammar Skills

Full Stops 1

Add full stops to this text:

My name is Tim I live in Nottingham, which is a city in the UK I live in a small detached house with my wife Jenny, and our two children, Lisa and James I work at Debenhams in Nottingham, and I really enjoy my job I am a sales manager for the sports clothing department Debenhams is the largest department store in Nottingham and there are branches all over the UK

When I'm not at work I like to play tennis with my friend Joe He is much better than me, but I still enjoy it At the weekends I sometimes take my family to Manchester to visit Jenny's mum She lives at Pine View Nursing Home in a nice suburb of the city and has been there for about five years She loves to see her grandchildren James always tells her about what he is doing at school James and Lisa both go to the same school, Mount Street Junior School

Test Your Grammar Skills
Full Stops 2

Add full stops to this text:

Hello, I'm Jenny, Tim's wife We have been married for almost eleven years I met Tim when we were both at university I studied Physics while Tim studied Business Management We graduated from Cardiff University in 1989, and went to live in Birmingham We got married in 1993 at Lincoln Cathedral I took a one-year post-graduate teaching course, then got a job teaching Science at Lincoln High School

We moved to Nottingham in 1996 where Lisa was born I remember that she was a very fat baby, but a happy one! My mum helped us with looking after the baby in the first year, before she had to go into the nursing home in Manchester She wanted to move to a home in Manchester because that is where my two older sisters and their families live We go to visit often - when I can get Tim to drive us up there! I don't drive I took some lessons when I was a student in Cardiff but I found driving on the roads quite frightening and gave up! Perhaps one day I will try again

About two years after we had Lisa, James was born He was born at St.Patrick's hospital in Nottingham It seems like it was only last week I can't believe he's already at school

Test Your Grammar Skills
Capital Letters 3

Put capital letters in the right places in this text:

my name is tim. i live in nottingham, which is a city in the uk. i live in a small detached house with my wife jenny, and our two children, lisa and james. i work at debenhams in nottingham, and i really enjoy my job. i am a sales manager for the sports clothing department. debenhams is the largest department store in nottingham and there are branches all over the uk.

when i'm not at work i like to play tennis with my friend joe. he is much better than me, but i still enjoy it. at the weekends i sometimes take my family to manchester to visit jenny's mum. she lives at pine view nursing home in a nice suburb of the city and has been there for about five years. she loves to see her grandchildren. james always tells her about what he is doing at school. james and lisa both go to the same school, mount street junior school.

Test Your Grammar Skills
Capital Letters 4

Put capital letters in the right places in this text:

hello, i'm jenny, tim's wife. we have been married for almost eleven years. i met tim when we were both at university. i studied physics while tim studied business management. we graduated from cardiff university in 1989, and went to live in birmingham. we got married in 1993 at lincoln cathedral. i took a one- year post-graduate teaching course, then got a job teaching science at lincoln high school.

we moved to nottingham in 1996 where lisa was born. i remember that she was a very fat baby, but a happy one! my mum helped us with looking after the baby in the first year, before she had to go into the nursing home in manchester. she wanted to move to a home in manchester because that is where my two older sisters and their families live. we go to visit often - when i can get tim to drive us up there! i don't drive. i took some lessons when i was a student in cardiff but i found driving on the roads quite frightening and gave up! perhaps one day i will try again.

about two years after we had lisa, james was born. he was born at st.patrick's hospital in nottingham. it seems like it was only last week. i can't believe he's already at school.

Test Your Grammar Skills

Past 1

Complete the sentences below using one of these verbs:

went	did
ate	had
watched	drank
was	heard
came	walked

1. I missed the bus so I _____home.

2. I_____some cereal and toast for my breakfast.

3. Last week I_____to London for the weekend.

4. I_____you talking about my friend yesterday.

5. Last night I_____a film about space travel.

6. I didn't go alone. My friend_____with me.

7. _____you enjoy the concert?

8. It _____raining this morning so I didn't go out.

9. I _____two glasses of water before going to bed.

10. I went to the shop to see if they_____any postcards.

Test Your Grammar Skills

Past 2

Complete the sentences below using one of these verbs:

went	did
laughed	had
made	tried
was	wanted
left	cooked

1. I _____a really nice meal for my mum's birthday.

2. My brother _____to come too, but he wasn't allowed.

3. We all _____when Tina fell off her chair!

4. I think that we were _____for each other.

5. Kim and Charlotte_____the party at 1.40am.

6. He _____to call you but couldn't get through.

7. I _____thinking of going to the coast next weekend.

8. _____you know that Tessa is getting married?

9. I went home after the concert _____finished.

10. My friends all _____to see the new exhibition in town.

Test Your Grammar Skills
Past Events
The Life of Captain James Cook

Complete the sentences below using one of these verbs:

saw	**joined**	**stayed**	**left**	**became**	**murdered**
landed	**married**	**born**	**buried**	**returned**	**departed**
arrived	**crossed**	**met**	**worked**	**promoted**	**hit**

1. James Cook was _____ on 27th October 1728.

2. He first _____ as an apprentice to a shopkeeper in Staithes, N. Yorkshire.

3. He _____ the Royal Navy in 1755, aged 26 years old.

4. He _____ Elizabeth Batts on 21st December 1762.

5. He _____ from his first voyage to Newfoundland as a surveyor in November 1763.

6. He was _____ to the rank of lieutenant in the Royal Navy in 1768.

7. He _____ from Plymouth in the Endeavour on 26th August 1768.

8. The Endeavour _____ at Tahiti on 11th April 1769.

9. Cook and his men _____ at Botany Bay (in Australia) on 28th April 1770.

10. The Endeavour _____ a coral reef, causing great problems, in June 1770.

11. Cook and his wife _____ with his father in Yorkshire in December 1771.

12. Cook _____ Plymouth in the Resolution for his second round-the-world voyage on 13th July 1772.

13. The Resolution _____ the Antarctic Circle for the first time in January 1773.

14. Cook _____ ill as the expedition neared Easter Island in February 1774.

15. When he arrived back in England in the summer of 1775 he _____ King George III.

16. Cook _____ the west coast of North America on 6th March 1778.

17. He was _____ in Hawaii on Valentine's Day 1779.

18. The remains of Cook's body were _____ in Kealakekua Bay on 22nd February 1779.

Test Your Grammar Skills
Second Conditional 1

If I were you,	I'd get my hair cut.
If I had the time,	I'd take up golf.
If I saw you more often,	we could get to know each other better.
If I lost my wallet,	I'd report it at the police station.
If I met Michael Jordan,	I'd ask him for his autograph.
If I won the lottery,	I'd buy a house for my brother.
If I wasn't so lazy,	I'd start my own business.
If my friend were here,	you could meet him.
If I drank too much,	I'd be sure to make a fool of myself.
If I studied more often,	I might get better grades.
If I woke up at nine am,	I'd be late for work.
If I entered the competition,	I wouldn't do very well.
If I played football for England,	they wouldn't keep losing!
If I saw my children smoking,	I'd be really angry with them.
If I came to class early,	I could finish my homework.

Test Your Grammar Skills

Second Conditional 2

If I bought a video recorder,	I wouldn't miss my favourite soap.
If I wore that red dress,	they would all notice me.
If I left it up to you,	we wouldn't get anything done.
If I had a word-processing package,	I could type up my reports.
If I were twenty years' younger,	I'd marry her!
If I needed help,	I would ask you.
If I moved to Canada,	I could get a good job out there.
If we took part in the quiz,	we might win it.
If we saw that film,	you wouldn't enjoy it.
If the computer crashed,	you'd lose all your unsaved work.
If our boat got lost,	we'd have to call for help.
If I told her that I'm a vegetarian,	she'd be surprised.
If my washing machine broke,	I'd get it mended.
If I had a heart attack,	I might die.
If I were Prime Minister,	I'd privatise the NHS.

Test Your Grammar Skills
Third Conditional 1

If you'd eaten your dinner,	you wouldn't have been hungry.
If I'd married Harry,	we would have been happy.
If I'd sold my car to you,	you'd have got a bargain.
If you'd attended every lesson,	you'd have passed that exam easily.
If it'd been sunny yesterday,	we would've gone to the beach.
If I'd told you about Chantal,	you wouldn't have believed me.
If we'd read the map properly,	we wouldn't have got lost.
If you'd asked her,	she could've come as well.
If I'd won the lottery,	I wouldn't be shopping in charity shops!
If you'd eaten all of your main course,	you could've had some dessert.
If I'd had the chance,	I would have gone to university.
If I'd had your phone number,	I could've called you.
If I'd asked the doctor,	she would've advised me on what to do.
If I'd lent you my lawnmower,	you would have broken it.
If I'd watched that programme	I would've been bored stiff.

Test Your Grammar Skills
Third Conditional 2

If I'd had the salmon,	I might have got food poisoning.
If I'd gone to the interview,	I might have got the job.
If they'd scored another goal,	they would've won.
If I'd found some money,	I would've handed it in.
If I'd taken a taxi,	I would have been there by now.
If I'd thrown away your magazine,	you would've been annoyed.
If I'd gone on the trip to London,	I would've visited Hyde Park.
If I'd eaten your chocolates,	I would've felt a bit guilty.
If I'd known it was your birthday,	I would've got you a present.
If we didn't remember which room it was,	we could've asked Stephen.
If the train had been late,	we would've missed our appointment.
If I'd had the courage,	I would've confronted her.
If I'd opened the shop on Sundays,	I would've compromised my beliefs.
If you'd been here earlier,	you could have had a free drink.
If my shirt had been dry,	I could have put it on.

Test Your Grammar Skills
Zero Conditional 1

If you heat water,	it boils.
If you put salt and vinegar on chips,	they taste nicer.
If you need assistance,	press here.
If you don't come on time,	you miss such a lot.
If you feel tired,	it's a good idea to go to bed.
If it rains,	it's good for the garden.
If I eat too many sweets,	I put on weight.
If I get up too early,	I feel tired all day.
If I have toothache,	I go to the dentist's.
If I feel ill,	I make an appointment with my GP.
If I read without my glasses on,	I strain my eyes.
If the number 54 is late,	the next bus is the 56.
If school finishes early,	I usually go to my friend's house.
If the post comes on time,	I look at it before I go to work.
If you spill coffee on my laptop,	it doesn't agree with it!

Test Your Grammar Skills
Zero Conditional 2

Soap dissolves	if you leave it in water.
Plants die	if you don't water them.
Milk goes off	if you don't keep it in a cool place.
Ask the teacher	if you don't understand.
I don't mind	if you want to use the car.
Children get upset	if they're being bullied.
Stamps can be good fun	if you enjoy collecting things.
It can be hard to access the web	if you don't have a PC at home.
The heater comes on	if you press this switch.
Pasta tastes awful	if you let it boil for too long.
I can go early on Fridays	if I ask my manager's permission.
I usually like listening to the radio	if Julie has it on.
My mind goes blank	if you put me on the spot.
The car runs like a dream	if you service it regularly.
Dogs really like it	if you walk them regularly.

Test Your Grammar Skills
Comparisons 1

Write a sentence comparing one thing with another. For example:
Compare two rooms in your house:
My bathroom is smaller than my living room.

1. Compare two people in your class:

_____

2. Compare two films that you have seen:

_____

3. Compare two Asian countries:

_____

4. Compare two types of transport:

_____

5. Compare two novels that you have read:

_____

6. Compare two places near to where you live:

_____

7. Compare two famous people from history:

_____

8. Compare two capital cities:

_____

9. Compare two occupations:

_____

10. Compare two days of the week:

_____

Test Your Grammar Skills
Comparisons 2

Write a sentence comparing one thing with another. For example:
Compare two animals: *An elephant is larger than a cat.*

1. Compare two teachers that you have had:

_____

2. Compare two television programmes:

_____

3. Compare two members of your family:

_____

4. Compare two European cities:

_____

5. Compare two types of music:

_____

6. Compare two places that you have visited on holiday:

_____

7. Compare two makes of car:

_____

8. Compare two planets in the Solar System:

_____

9. Compare two restaurants that you know:

_____

10. Compare two languages:

_____

English Fundamentals Worksheet
Homophones 1

*Homophones are words that sound the same as each other,
but have different spellings and meanings.
Write an English word that sounds the same as each of these words:*

1   allowed   _____

2   jeans   _____

3   father   _____

4   tide   _____

5   peace   _____

6   see   _____

7   weather   _____

8   you   _____

9   pour   _____

10   none   _____

11   hear   _____

12   floor   _____

13   by   _____

14   cereal   _____

15   vein   _____

English Fundamentals Worksheet
Homophones 2

Homophones are words that sound the same as each other, but have different spellings and meanings.
Write an English word that sounds the same as each of these words:

1 stair _____

2 need _____

3 pear _____

4 wear _____

5 road _____

6 made _____

7 dual _____

8 beech _____

9 aunt _____

10 feet _____

11 for _____

12 lane _____

13 idle _____

14 great _____

15 bass _____

English Fundamentals Worksheet
Homophones List

Homophones are words that sound the same as each other, but have different spellings and meanings. Here are some common examples:

allowed	aloud	eight	ate	lead	led	saw	sore
aunt	aren't	faint	feint	least	leased	see	sea
ball	bawl	farther	father	loan	lone	sun	son
base	bass	feet	feat	male	mail	tail	tale
be	bee	find	fined	no	know	tea	tee
bear	bare	flair	flare	meet	meat	their	they're
berry	bury	floor	flaw	mind	mined	they're	there
blue	blew	flower	flour	morning	mourning	tide	tied
boar	bore	for	four	naval	navel	too	to
board	bored	fur	fir	new	knew	two	too
bread	bred	great	grate	one	won	wail	whale
buy	by	hart	heart	pear	pair	warn	worn
by	bye	heal	heel	pie	pi	weal	wheel
cereal	serial	hear	here	piece	peace	wear	where
check	cheque	heard	herd	pier	peer	weather	whether
council	counsel	hi	high	poor	pour	week	weak
course	coarse	hole	whole	rain	reign	weight	wait
dam	damn	idle	idol	raw	roar	while	wile
deer	dear	in	inn	read	reed	wood	would
die	dye	it's	its	red	read	write	right
doe	dough	jeans	genes	road	rode	yew	you
earn	urn	lane	lain	sale	sail	your	you're

Test Your Grammar Skills
Being Polite

*We are usually more **polite** to people who we respect or who we don't know well. We tend to use more **direct** language with our friends and close relatives. Match the **polite** sentence with the **direct** sentence that has the same meaning:*

Polite:

1. Can I have a cake?

2. Would you be able to keep the noise down please?

3. Can you pass me the lemonade please?

4. Would you like to sit down?

5. Can you tell me how long you are going to be please?

6. I wondered if I would possibly be able to borrow the newspaper after you have finished with it.

7. Excuse me. I'm afraid I don't know your name.

8. I'm sorry but I've got to go home now.

9. Would you mind if I came with you and Diane to the cinema?

10. Excuse me. I'm ever so sorry to bother you. I hope you don't mind but would it be possible at all for you to tell me the time please?

Direct:

a) Sit down.

b) Get a move on. c) Who are you?

d) What's the time?

e) Give me a cake.

f) I'm coming with you. g) Give me a drink.

h) I want the paper now!

i) Shut up!

j) I'm off.

Test Your Grammar Skills
Good Advice 1

Match the question on the left to the good advice given on the right:

1. Are you hungry?   a) Go to the doctor's!

2. Are you unhappy?   b) Have something to eat!

3. Are you bored?   c) Go and work in a hospital!

4. Are you tired?   d) Go for a ten mile run!

5. Are you in a hurry?   e) Have something to drink!

6. Are you feeling ill?   f) Go and buy some!

7. Are you lonely?   g) Go to bed!

8. Are you thirsty?   h) Cheer up - it might never happen!

9. Do you need some new shoes?   i) Go and sit in a field!

10. Do you need a new suit?   j) Go and get one!

11. Do you feel stressed out?   k) Make some friends!

12. Do you like boats?   l) Go and do something!

13. Do you like trees and grass?   m) Go and buy a lottery ticket!

14. Do you like ill people?   n) Go on a sailing holiday!

15. Do you want to be a millionaire? o) Stop eating chocolate and cakes!

16. Do you want to be famous?   p) Start by making others happy.

17. Do you want to be happy?   q) Slow down a bit!

18. Do you like mountains?   r) Get a part in a Hollywood blockbuster!

19. Are you unfit?   s) Go to the Himalayas!

20. Do you want to lose weight?   t) Calm down!

Test Your Grammar Skills
Good Advice 2

Match the question on the left to the good advice given on the right:

1. Do you like meeting people?   a) Good for you!

2. Do you like cars?   b) Get a job as a receptionist!

3. Are you very shy?   c) Become a racing driver.

4. Are you looking for romance?   d) Go and visit St Paul's Cathedral.

5. Are you lucky in love?   e) Go to the hairdressers!

6. Do you want to be poor?   f) Put some gloves on!

7. Do you like pop music?   g) Go and buy some new plants!

8. Do you like watching films?   h) Go and work in a garage!

9. Do you need help with maths?   i) Go to a nice restaurant!

10. Have you got long hair?   j) Buy a calculator!

11. Have you got cold hands?   k) Give all your money away!

12. Do you like good food?   l) Go on holiday to Spain!

13. Do you like gardening?   m) Phone somebody!

14. Do you live in London?   n) Switch on the TV!

15. Do you like flying?   o) Join a dating agency!

16. Do you like talking?   p) Go on a confidence-building course.

17. Do you know how to read a map?   q) Get a job as a film reviewer.

18. Do you like lying in the sun all day? r) Buy a couple of CDs.

19. Do you like watching TV?   s) Become an air hostess!

20. Do you like driving really fast?   t) Go on a walking holiday!

Test Your Grammar Skills
Good Advice 3

Match the question on the left to the good advice given on the right:

1. Do you like looking good?   a) Take off your jumper!

2. Do you like jam?   b) Go to Panama!

3. Are you dirty?   c) Move to a smaller one!

4. Have you got long hair?   d) Buy a cow!

5. Do you always wake up late?   e) Buy a better one!

6. Do you hate your job?   f) Make yourself a jam sandwich!

7. Is your house too big?   g) Go to the Sahara Desert!

8. Do you like drinking fresh milk?   h) Why not get it cut?

9. Do you enjoy swimming?   i) Go to a birthday party!

10. Do you like penguins?   j) Go to a carpet shop!

11. Are you too hot?   k) Join a tennis club!

12. Are you too cold?   l) Buy some big shoes!

13. Do you like long canals?   m) Buy an alarm clock!

14. Do you like sand dunes?   n) Become a model.

15. Do you like birthday cake?   o) Go to the South Pole!

16. Do you like getting wet?   p) Put a warm coat on!

17. Do you need a new carpet?   q) Go on a boat trip and jump in!

18. Do you like playing tennis?   r) Have a bath!

19. Do you have big feet?   s) Apply for a different one!

20. Is your mobile phone rubbish?   t) Throw away your umbrella!

English Fundamentals Worksheet
Write Your Own Flashcards

The answers
Part One

Basic English Written Test
Sunday, Monday, Tuesday, Wednesday, Thursday, Friday, Saturday;
January, February, March, April, May, June, July, August, September,
October, November, December;
one, two, three, four, five, six, seven, eight, nine, ten, eleven, twelve,
thirteen, fourteen, fifteen, sixteen, seventeen, eighteen, nineteen, twenty,
twenty onc, twenty two, twenty three, twenty four, twenty five, twenty
six, twenty seven, twenty eight, twenty nine, thirty.

Vocabulary Test
This blank form can be used to test spelling skills and vocabulary within
a wide variety of vocabulary sets. Students have to write a word that
belongs to a given set, beginning with each letter of the alphabet. For
example, you could ask them to write an adjective, or an occupation, for
every letter of the alphabet.

Just Vowels - Days, Months and Seasons 1
1. Friday. 2. October. 3. Thursday. 4. April. 5. February. 6. Monday.
7. Saturday. 8. autumn. 9. January. 10. November. 11. March. 12.
June.

Just Vowels - Days, Months and Seasons 2
1. Sunday. 2. spring. 3. Wednesday. 4. December. 5. summer. 6. July.
7. winter. 8. May. 9. September. 10. August. 11. Tuesday.

Days of the Week
1. a) 2. c) 3. d) 4. b) 5. a) 6. b) 7. d)

Months of the Year
1. b) 2. a) 3. c) 4. a) 5. d) 6. b) 7. c) 8. a) 9. b) 10. d) 11. b) 12. d)

Understanding Dates 1

1. the 1st of January 1997;
2. the 5th of June 1983;
3. the10th of July 2002;
4. the 14th of August 2012;
5. the 22nd of November 2001;
6. the 31st of December 2003;
7. the 3rd of February 1990;
8. the 17th of January 2000;
9. the 27th of March 1995;
10. the 20th of April 2009;
11. the 30th of October 2001;
12. the 9th of June 2011;
13. the13th of September 2002;
14. the 2nd of November 1993;
15. the 1st of January 2000.

Understanding Dates 2

1. the 2nd of January 1999;
2. the 1st of February 2003;
3. the 16th of September 1997;
4. the 2nd of March 2005;
5. the 1st of March 2004;
6. the 4th of August 2011;
7. the 10th of February 1996;
8. the 15th of December 2001;
9. the 29th of October 2002;
10. the 2nd of February 1996;
11. the 14th of May 2012;
12. the 1st of May 2001;
13. the 12th of November 1998;
14. the 15th of January 1995;
15. the 4th of August 2010.

Common Irregular Verbs 1

to be: I am, You are, He is, She is, It is, We are, They are.

to go: I go, You go, He goes, She goes, It goes, We go, They go.

to do: I do, You do, He does, She does, It does, We do, They do.

to have: I have, You have, He has, She has, It has, We have, They have.

Common Irregular Verbs 2

to be: I was, You were, He was, She was, It was, We were, They were.

to go: I went, You went, He went, She went, It went, We went, They went.

to do: I did, You did, He did, She did, It did, We did, They did.

to have: I had, You had, He had, She had, It had, We had, They had.

Common Irregular Verbs 3

to be: I am being, You are being, He is being, She is being, It is being, We are being, They are being.

to go: I am going, You are going, He is going, She is going, It is going, We are going, They are going.

to do: I am doing, You are doing, He is doing, She is doing, It is doing, We are doing, They are doing.

to have: I am having, You are having, He is having, She is having, It is having, We are having, They are having.

Using Capital Letters 1

The following should start with a capital letter: John, England, Pizza Hut, Monday, New York, January, Sarah, King Edward High School, Atlantic Ocean, December, French.

Using Capital Letters 2

The following should start with a capital letter: Claire, Spain, Mount Everest, Indian, Paris, August, Steven, Doctor I P Jones, Burger King, Manchester General Hospital, Wednesday.

Basic Sentence Punctuation 1

1. My sister's name is Jackie.
2. Friday is my favourite day of the week.
3. I like watching Eastenders on BBC 1.
4. Charles Dickens was a famous writer. He was born in Portsmouth.
5. Lisa and Chantal are going on holiday to Portugal in May.
6. Did you go to school today?
7. My new address is 248 Normanton Road in Nottingham.
8. When are you going to the hospital?
9. My doctor is getting a new receptionist. She's called Louise Robson.
10. Ben and I are going to look around Leicester Grammar School on Wednesday.

Basic Sentence Punctuation 2

1. How do I get to the library from here?
2. The coach for London leaves in about half an hour.
3. My birthday is in September. I usually go out for a drink with my friends.
4. What do you want for dinner tonight?
5. Birmingham is the second largest city in the UK.
6. I'll have a Coke please and two packets of Walkers crisps.
7. If you need to see a consultant go to the Derbyshire Royal Infirmary.
8. Mary Poppins is my mum's favourite film. She likes Julie Andrews.
9. I drive a red Fiat Punto and my uncle drives a green BMW.
10. I joined Morton Park Golf Club last week. It was very expensive.

Question Forms Using Verb 'to be' (Present Simple Tense) 1

1. What is your brother's name?
2. What is your address?
3. What is your favourite food?
4. What is your name?
5. What is the date today?
6. How much is that shirt?
7. How are you?
8. What is your surname?
9. What is your postcode?
10. When is your birthday?

Question Forms Using Verb 'to be' (Present Simple Tense) 2
1. Where are the toilets?
2. Where are you from?
3. What is your phone number?
4. What is the answer?
5. What is your nationality?
6. How old is it?
7. Who is your best friend?
8. Which one is it?
9. Where is my shirt?
10. How old are you?

Question Forms Using Verb 'to be' (Present Simple Tense) 3
1. What is your first name?
2. What is the capital of Australia?
3. Is that your friend's car?
4. Is it cold outside?
5. When is the concert?
6. Are his parents nice?
7. How many people are there in your class?
8. What is your favourite colour?
9. When was the Battle of Hastings?
10. Are you OK?

Question Forms Using Verb 'to do' as an Auxiliary Verb (Present Simple Tense) 1
1. What do you do in your free time?
2. Where do you live?
3. How do you do?
4. How do you get there?
5. What do you do for a living?
6. What do you think?
7. What do you want?
8. Who do you want to speak to?
9. Where do you want to go?
10. Do you know him?

Question Forms Using Verb 'to do' as an Auxiliary Verb (Present Simple Tense) 2

1. Do you have to ask?
2. When do you want to have lunch?
3. Do you have any stamps?
4. Do you have any brothers and sisters?
5. Where do you work?
6. What do you want for breakfast?
7. Who do you think you are?
8. Which newspapers do you read?
9. Why do you like playing snooker?
10. Do you want some fish and chips?

Question Forms Using Verb 'to do' as an Auxiliary Verb (Present Simple Tense) 3

1. Where do you come from?
2. Do you think English is boring?
3. Which one do you like best?
4. What do they want to know?
5. Do you feel OK?
6. Does she enjoy watching old films?
7. Does Louis work hard?
8. Do you want to start this course?
9. Do you know the way to the library?
10. Do you want me to come with you?

Question Forms Using Verb 'to have' as an Auxiliary Verb (Present Perfect Tense) 1

1. Where have you been?
2. What have you been doing?
3. Why have you come to this class?
4. When have I got to arrive?
5. Have you got any money?
6. Have you got the time please?
7. Have you seen my friend?
8. Have you looked in every cupboard?
9. Have you closed the curtains?
10. Why hasn't she done the washing up?

Question Forms Using Verb 'to have' as an Auxiliary Verb (Present Perfect Tense) 2

1. Have you been here before?
2. Which films have you seen?
3. Have you got any oranges?
4. Have you had your tea?
5. Have you finished with that magazine?
6. Has he told you that I'm leaving?
7. Have you got your certificate yet?
8. Have you changed your phone number?
9. What have you learnt today?
10. Have you bought a birthday card for Jane?

Question Forms Using Verb 'to have' as an Auxiliary Verb (Present Perfect Tense) 3

1. When have you got to go?
2. Why hasn't he finished painting the bathroom?
3. Have you finished your meal?
4. Have you heard the new CD by Bon Jovi?
5. What have they been saying to you?
6. What have you done to your hair?
7. What has he done with my photos?
8. Where have they been on holiday?
9. Who has she been talking to?
10. Why haven't you tidied up?

Elementary Homophones 1
1. find. 2. knows. 3. be. 4. its. 5. mail. 6. board. 7. mourning. 8. by. 9. high. 10. bare. 11. meet. 12. dear. 13. for. 14. heel. 15. aren't.

Elementary Homophones 2
1. pail. 2. one. 3. mind. 4. no. 5. loan. 6. pear. 7. plane. 8. new. 9. read. 10. poor. 11. piece. 12. night. 13. none. 14. raise. 15. or.

Part Two

Using Numbers 1

1. fourteen. 2. forty two. 3. two. 4. fifteen. 5. three. 6. eighty. 7. sixty. 8. four. 9. six. 10. thirty. 11. thirty seven. 12. fifty three.

Using Numbers 2

1. sixteen. 2. forty three. 3. thirty eight. 4. minus nine (-9). 5. thirty five. 6. one hundred and forty five. 7. forty eight. 8. eleven. 9. fifteen. 10. two hundred and seventy five. 11. eighty four. 12. sixty seven.

Using Numbers 3

a) twelve; twenty seven; sixty eight; sixty three; one hundred and eighty nine.

b) twelve; eight; forty; fifty seven; forty two.

c) eighty; ninety eight; one hundred and fifty six; one hundred and forty six; five hundred and eighty four.

Using Numbers 4

a) twelve; twenty; nineteen; one hundred and seventy one; one hundred and seventy eight.

b) fifty five; twenty five; seventy five; fifty seven; sixty nine.

c) seventy six; one hundred and thirty nine; one hundred and ten; one hundred and twenty; four hundred and eighty.

Using Numbers 5

a) sixteen; thirty seven; seventy two; sixty four; six hundred and forty.

b) seventy one; sixty five; fifty three; two hundred and twelve; two thousand three hundred and eighteen.

c) one thousand one hundred and forty nine; one thousand one hundred and fifty three; one thousand and seventy two; two thousand one hundred and forty four; six thousand seven hundred and nineteen.

Working Out Prices 1
1. six pounds forty nine pence.
2. fifteen pounds nineteen pence.
3. fourteen pounds sixty seven pence.
4. thirty seven pounds eighty five pence.
5. eight pounds eighty eight pence.
6. three hundred and forty six pounds fifty one pence.
7. six pounds fifty pence.
8. thirteen pounds fifty pence.
9. four pounds forty nine pence.
10. nine pounds seventy six pence.
11. forty two pounds seventy one pence.
12. thirty six pounds eleven pence.

Working Out Prices 2
1. six pounds eighty pence.
2. twenty two pounds forty nine pence.
3. eight pounds ninety seven pence.
4. eighteen pounds.
5. forty two pounds ninety eight pence.
6. twenty five pence.
7. twenty six pounds forty five pence.
8. one pound twenty seven pence.
9. eleven pounds forty three pence.
10. one hundred and twenty eight pounds ninety seven pence.
11. sixty seven pence.
12. one pound seven pence.

Ordinals 1 - Months of the Year
1. tenth. 2. first. 3. fourth. 4. third. 5. ninth. 6. sixth. 7. fifth. 8. second. 9. twelfth. 10. seventh. 11. eleventh. 12. eighth.

Ordinals 2 - The Alphabet
1. first. 2. sixteenth. 3. fifth. 4. twenty fourth.5. twelfth. 6. twentieth.
7. fifteenth. 8. thirteenth. 9. sixth. 10. seventh. 11. eleventh.
12. eighteenth. 13. twenty first. 14. fourth. 15. tenth.

Opposite Adjectives 1

clever/stupid; poor/rich; sunny/rainy; wet/dry; long/short; fat/thin; big/small; good/bad; hard/soft; low/high.

Opposite Adjectives 2

light/dark; warm/cool; old/young; odd/normal; fast/slow; expensive/cheap; hungry/full; uneven/flat; wide/narrow; tall/short.

Comparatives and Superlatives 1

1. lighter, lightest. 2. cleverer, cleverest. 3. sunnier, sunniest.
4. harder, hardest. 5. thinner, thinnest. 6. better, best. 7. poorer, poorest.
8. shorter, shortcst. 9. later, latest. 10. happier, happiest.

Comparatives and Superlatives 2

1. shadier, shadiest. 2. stupider, stupidest. 3. rainier, rainiest.
4. softer, softest. 5. fatter, fattest. 6. worse, worst. 7. richer, richest.
8. longer, longest. 9. earlier, earliest. 10. sadder, saddest.

Note: worksheets **Comparatives and Superlatives 1 & 2** can be used together to teach opposite adjectives, e.g. light is the opposite of shady.

Comparatives and Superlatives 3

1. nicer, nicest. 2. colder, coldest. 3. cleaner, cleanest.
4. younger, youngest. 5. faster, fastest. 6. larger, largest.
7. hungrier, hungriest. 8. narrower, narrowest. 9. redder, reddest.
10. nearer, nearest.

Comparatives and Superlatives 4

1. nastier, nastiest. 2. hotter, hottest. 3. dirtier, dirtiest. 4. older, oldest.
5. slower, slowest. 6. smaller, smallest. 7. fuller, fullest. 8. wider, widest. 9. greener, greenest. 10. further, furthest or farther, farthest.

Note: worksheets **Comparatives and Superlatives 3 & 4** can be used together to teach opposite adjectives, e.g. nice is the opposite of nasty.

Using Indefinite Articles 1

1. a; 2. a; 3. a; 4. an; 5. an; 6. an; 7. an; 8. a; 9. a; 10. a; 11. an; 12. an; 13. a; 14. a; 15. a.

Using Indefinite Articles 2

1. an; 2. an; 3. a; 4. an; 5. a; 6. a; 7. a; 8. an; 9. an; 10. an; 11. a; 12. a; 13. an; 14. a; 15. a.

Countable and Uncountable Nouns 1

some sand; a five pound note; some wine; some butter; some peanut butter; a radio; a toothbrush; some jam; a magazine; a queue; some luggage; a suitcase; some flour; some sugar; a bicycle.

Countable and Uncountable Nouns 2

some rice; a dog; a postman; some alcohol; a bathroom; a computer; some oil; some ice; a shirt; some homework; some food; some cheese; a light switch; some vinegar; a pen.

Part Three

Using Personal Pronouns 1

1. me. 2. I. 3. me. 4. Me. 5. I. 6. I. 7. I. 8. me. 9. me. 10. I. 11. me. 12. I. 13. me. 14. me. 15. I.

Using Personal Pronouns 2

1. He. 2. him. 3. He. 4. He. 5. him. 6. him. 7. He. 8. he. 9. him. 10. He. 11. He. 12. him. 13. him. 14. him. 15. him.

Using Personal Pronouns 3

1. She. 2. She. 3. her. 4. her. 5. her. 6. she. 7. She. 8. She. 9. her. 10. she. 11. She. 12. her, her. 13. She. 14. she. 15. she.

Using Personal Pronouns 4

1. We. 2. us. 3. us. 4. we. 5. we. 6. us. 7. We. 8. us. 9. We. 10. we. 11. We. 12. us. 13. us. 14. We, we. 15. us.

Using Personal Pronouns 5
1. them. 2. They. 3. them. 4. them. 5. They. 6. them, they. 7. them.
8. them. 9. They. 10. they. 11. them. 12. them, they. 13. They, them.
14. them, they. 15. they.

Using Personal Pronouns 6
1. He. 2. you. 3. He, me. 4. it, you. 5. us. 6. she, them. 7. you, me.
8. It, him. 9. them. 10. me.

Using Personal Pronouns 7
11. It. 12. him, they. 13. I, it. 14. He, it. 15. it. 16. She, me. 17. you.
18. her, He, her, he. 19. They. 20. him.

Adverbs of Frequency 1
There may be some discussion about what is right or wrong! The percentages should look something like this: 100% always, 90% usually, 80% frequently, 70% often, 50% sometimes, 30% don't usually, 15% seldom, 10% occasionally, 5% hardly ever, 0% never.

First Conditional 1,2
Copy this page onto card. It shows fifteen sentences that use a conditional clause. Cut up the cards and get your students to match up both parts of each sentence correctly. You could also show only one half of each sentence and elicit ideas on how to complete the sentences.

'Wh - ' Questions 1
1. What. 2. What. 3. Who. 4. Where. 5. When. 6. Why. 7. When.
8. What. 9. What. 10. Why. 11. Who. 12. Why. 13. Where. 14. Where.
15. When.

'Wh - ' Questions 2
1. Where. 2. Who. 3. What. 4. Why. 5. When. 6. When. 7. Where.
8. Who. 9. When. 10. Why. 11. What. 12. Who. 13. What. 14. Where.
15. Why.

Compound Nouns 1
afternoon, birthday, bookshelf, tabletop, airport, teatime, pancake, paperback, caveman, horsefly, parenthood homework, carpet, cupboard.

Compound Nouns 2
timetable, bathroom, inside, outhouse, nobody, cliffhanger, policewoman, sometimes, breadbin, anteater, waterfall, wheelbarrow, fallout, daybreak.

Compound Nouns 3
lampshade, wheelchair, football, invalid, humankind, shoplifter, fireman, footage, motorbike, butterfly, railway, miniskirt, namesake, tracksuit.

Daily Routines 1
I wake up at 7.05am.
I get up at 7.15am.
I have/take a shower at 7.30am.
I have/eat breakfast at 7.45am.
I read the newspaper at 8.00am.
I catch a bus to work at 8.30am.
I start/begin work at 9.00am.
I have/take a coffee break at 10.30am.
I have/eat lunch at 1.00pm.

Daily Routines 2
I talk to my friend on the phone at 2.30pm.
I send/write/read an email at 2.40pm.
I go home at 5.00pm.
I have/eat dinner at 6.00pm.
I wash the dishes at 6.30pm.
I play football at 7.00pm.
I watch TV at 8.30pm.
I play my guitar at 9.00pm.
I read a book at 10.00pm.
I listen to the radio at 10.40pm.
I go to bed at 11.10pm.
I go to sleep at about 11.20pm.

Complete the Sentences 1

1. c) 2. c) 3. b) 4. d) 5. d) 6. a) 7. d) 8. b) 9. c) 10. a)

Complete the Sentences 2

1. a) 2. c) 3. b) 4. c) 5. b) 6. c) 7. b) 8. b) 9. b) 10. d)

Complete the Sentences 3

11. c) 12. c) 13. d) 14. b) 15. d) 16. b) 17. c) 18. b) 19. d) 20. c)

Complete the Sentences 4

1. b) 2. c) 3. b) 4. b) 5. c) 6. d) 7. b) 8. c) 9. c) 10. c)

Complete the Sentences 5

11. d) 12. c) 13. b) 14. d) 15. c) 16. d) 17. b) 18. b) 19. a) 20. c)

Complete the Sentences 6

1. d) 2. b) 3. b) 4. c) 5. d) 6. a) 7. b) 8. c) 9. b) 10. c)

Complete the Sentences 7

11. a) 12. b) 13. a) 14. c) 15. c) 16. d) 17. b) 18. a) 19. c) 20. a)

Complete the Sentences 8

1. c) 2. b) 3. d) 4. b) 5. a) 6. c) 7. b) 8. a) 9. d) 10. b)

Complete the Sentences 9

11. d) 12. b) 13. c) 14. c) 15. d) 16. a) 17. b) 18. c) 19. a) 20. c)

Complete the Sentences 10

1. d) 2. b) 3. a) 4. d) 5. c) 6. c) 7. a) 8. d) 9. b) 10. d)

Complete the Sentences 11

11. c) 12. d) 13. c) 14. b) 15. a) 16. b) 17. d) 18. b) 19. a) 20. c)

Sentence Building 1

1. My dog needs to go on a diet. 2. I went to my friend's house last night. 3. I would like to live near the seashore. 4. If I had some money I would buy a car. 5. It was my birthday last Saturday. 6. I live in a three-bedroomed house. 7. I need to buy some new curtains. 8. On Monday I am going on holiday to Spain.

Sentence Building 2

1. I need a stamp for my letter. 2. Can you tell me the time please? 3. I don't like spaghetti but I like pizza. Or: I like spaghetti but I don't like pizza. 4. My favourite book is Oliver Twist by Dickens. 5. On Sunday my sister came to see us. 6. I felt tired so I went to bed early. 7. Everybody else was at the party. 8. Would you like to go on holiday with them?

The Plays of William Shakespeare

a) "To be, or not to be, that is the question." Hamlet, Act 3 Scene 1, spoken by Hamlet.

b) "If music be the food of love, play on." Twelfth Night, Act 1 Scene 1, spoken by Duke Orsino.

c) "That which hath made them drunk hath made me bold." Macbeth, Act 2 Scene 2, spoken by Lady Macbeth.

d) "What hempen homespuns have we swaggering here?" A Midsummer Night's Dream, Act 3 Scene 1, spoken by Puck.

e) "But yet thou art my flesh, my blood, my daughter." King Lear, Act 2 Scene 4, spoken by King Lear.

f) "Thy husband is thy lord, thy life, thy keeper." Taming of the Shrew, Act 5 Scene 2, spoken by Katherine.

g) "Once more unto the breach, dear friends, once more." Henry V, Act 3 Scene 1, spoken by King Henry.

h) "A horse! A horse! My kingdom for a horse!" Richard III, Act 5 Scene 4, spoken by King Richard.

Part Four

Full Stops 1 & Using Capital Letters 3

My name is Tim. I live in Nottingham, which is a city in the UK. I live in a small detached house with my wife Jenny, and our two children, Lisa and James. I work at Debenhams in Nottingham, and I really enjoy my job. I am a sales manager for the sports clothing department. Debenhams is the largest department store in Nottingham and there are branches all over the UK.

When I'm not at work I like to play tennis with my friend Joe. He is much better than me, but I still enjoy it. At the weekends I sometimes take my family to Manchester to visit Jenny's mum. She lives at Pine View Nursing Home in a nice suburb of the city and has been there for about five years. She loves to see her grandchildren. James always tells her about what he is doing at school. James and Lisa both go to the same school, Mount Street Junior School.

Full Stops 2 & Using Capital Letters 4

Hello, I'm Jenny, Tim's wife. We have been married for almost eleven years. I met Tim when we were both at university. I studied Physics while Tim studied Business Management. We graduated from Cardiff University in 1989, and went to live in Birmingham. We got married in 1993 at Lincoln Cathedral. I took a one-year post- graduate teaching course, then got a job teaching Science at Lincoln High School.

We moved to Nottingham in 1996 where Lisa was born. I remember that she was a very fat baby, but a happy one! My mum helped us with looking after the baby in the first year, before she had to go into the nursing home in Manchester. She wanted to move to a home in Manchester because that is where my two older sisters and their families live. We go to visit often - when I can get Tim to drive us up there! I don't drive. I took some lessons when I was a student in Cardiff but I found driving on the roads quite frightening and gave up! Perhaps one day I will try again.

About two years after we had Lisa, James was born. He was born at St. Patrick's hospital in Nottingham. It seems like it was only last week. I can't believe he's already at school.

Talking about the Past 1
1. walked. 2. ate. 3. went. 4. heard. 5. watched. 6. came. 7. Did.
8. was. 9. drank. 10. had.

Talking about the Past 2
1. cooked. 2. wanted. 3. laughed. 4. made. 5. left. 6. tried. 7. was.
8. Did. 9. had. 10. went.

Past Events - The Life of Captain James Cook
1. born. 2. worked. 3. joined. 4. married. 5. returned. 6. promoted.
7. departed. 8. arrived. 9. landed. 10. hit. 11. stayed. 12. left.
13. crossed. 14. became. 15. met. 16. saw. 17. murdered. 18. buried.

Second Conditional 1,2; Third Conditional 1,2; Zero Conditional 1,2
Copy this page onto card. It shows fifteen sentences that use a
conditional clause. Cut up the cards and get your students to match up
both parts of each sentence correctly. You could also show only one half
of each sentence and elicit ideas on how to complete the sentences.

Writing Comparisons 1
Answers will vary. Here are some sample sentences: 1. Tina is taller
than Abid. 2. I like Rocky II better than Rocky III. 3. India has a bigger
population that South Korea. 4. Cars are more expensive to run than
bicycles. 5. Great Expectations is much better than Pride and Prejudice.
6. The park is further away from my house than the school. 7. Napoleon
is more interesting than Lord Nelson. 8. It is colder in Helsinki than it is
in Cairo. 9. Doctors get paid a lot more than mechanics. 10. Friday is
nearer to the weekend than Monday!

Writing Comparisons 2
Answers will vary. Here are some sample sentences: 1. My French
teacher is taller than my Maths teacher. 2. I prefer Coronation Street to
Eastenders. 3. My sister spends much longer in the bathroom than my
dad. 4. I have been to Madrid, but I've never been to Barcelona. 5.
Rock music is usually louder than folk music. 6. Wales is a far wetter
place than Cornwall. 7. A Ferrari can go faster than my Corsa. 8. Venus
is closer to the sun than Pluto. 9. Ricardo's Ristorante is more
expensive than Clifford's Café. 10. English is a more difficult language
to learn than Spanish.

Homophones 1

1. aloud. 2. genes. 3. farther. 4. tied. 5. piece. 6. sea. 7. whether. 8. ewe. 9. poor, pore. 10. nun. 11. here. 12. flaw. 13. buy. 14. serial. 15. vain.

Homophones 2

1. stare. 2. knead. 3. pair, pare. 4. where. 5. rode. 6. maid. 7. duel. 8. beach. 9. aren't. 10. feat. 11. four, fore. 12. lain. 13. idol. 14. grate. 15. base.

Being Polite

1. e) 2. i) 3. g) 4. a) 5. b) 6. h) 7. c) 8. j) 9. f) 10. d)

Good Advice 1

1. b) 2. h) 3. l) 4. g) 5. q) 6. a) 7. k) 8. e) 9. f) 10. j) 11. t) 12. n) 13. i) 14. c) 15. m) 16. r) 17. p) 18. s) 19. d) 20. o)

Good Advice 2

1. b) 2. h) 3. p) 4. o) 5. a) 6. k) 7. r) 8. q) 9. j) 10. e) 11. f) 12. i) 13. g) 14. d) 15. s) 16. m) 17. t) 18. l) 19. n) 20. c)

Good Advice 3

1. n) 2. f) 3. r) 4. h) 5. m) 6. s) 7. c) 8. d) 9. q) 10. o) 11. a) 12. p) 13. b) 14. g) 15. i) 16. t) 17. j) 18. k) 19. l) 20. e)

Made in the USA
Columbia, SC
16 January 2024